Come Home with Me
A Multicultural Treasure Hunt

A Kids Bridge Book
from The Children's Museum, Boston

This book series is based on The Kids Bridge exhibit created by Joanne Jones-Rizzi and Aylette Jenness, which was designed to help children understand and appreciate cultural diversity and work against prejudice and discrimination. Exhibit team: Fabiana Chiu, Brad Larson, Dan Spock, John Spalvins, Signe Hanson, and Dorothy Merrill.

by Aylette Jenness

Illustrated and designed by Laura DeSantis

Photographs by Max Belcher

Video frames by D'Arcy Marsh

THE NEW PRESS
New York, NY

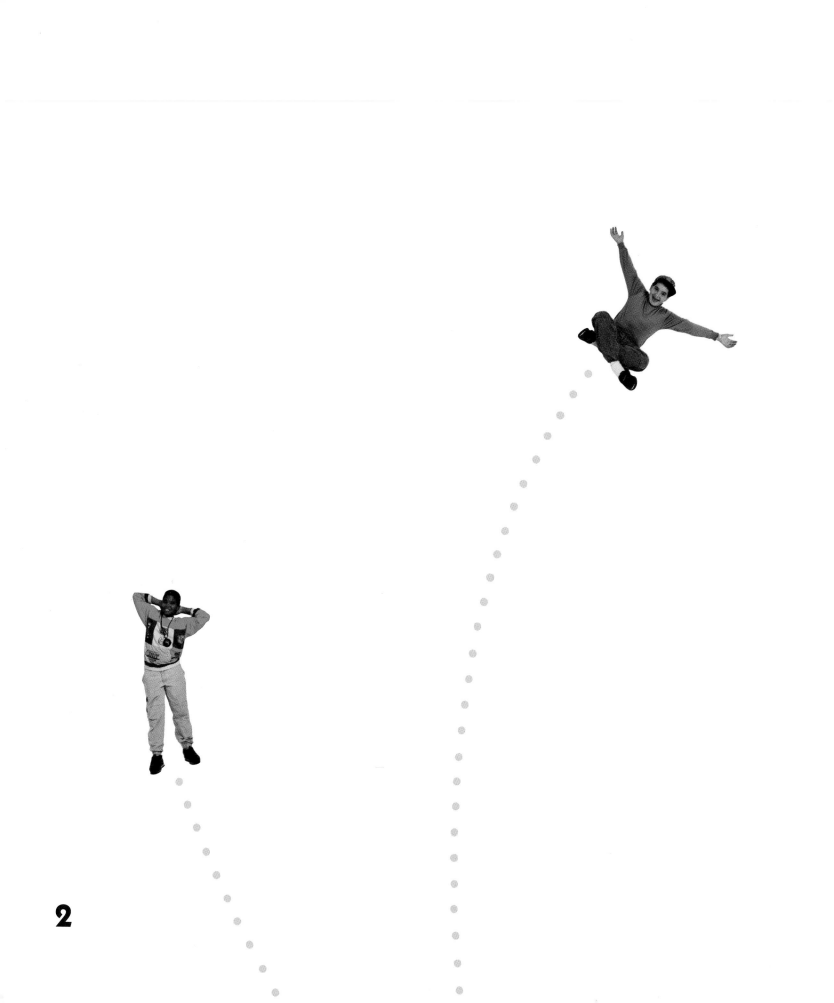

2

To Terri, Abdus, Annie, and Marco,
who opened their doors and
shared their lives with us.

3

THE NEW PRESS
New York, NY

Published in the United States by The New Press, New York
Distributed by W. W. Norton & Company, Inc.
500 Fifth Avenue, New York, NY 10110

LIBRARY OF CONGRESS CATALOGING-IN-PUBLICATION DATA

Jenness, Aylette.
Come home with me : a multicultural treasure hunt /
by Aylette Jenness. — 1st ed.
p.   cm.
ISBN 1-56584-064-X
1. Ethnic groups—Juvenile literature. 2. Ethnic attitudes—
Juvenile literature. 3. Toleration—Juvenile literature.
I. Title.
GN495.4.J45   1993
305.8—dc20
92-50699

First Edition
Designed by Laura DeSantis

Established in 1990 as a major alternative to the large, commercial publishing
houses, The New Press is intended to be the first full-scale nonprofit American
book publisher outside of the university presses. The Press is operated
editorially in the public interest, rather than for private gain. It is committed
to publishing in innovative ways works of educational, cultural, and
community value, which despite their intellectual merits might not
normally be "commercially viable."

Acknowledgments

Dozens of people from Boston's communities and The Children's Museum worked on The Kids Bridge exhibit and so made invaluable contributions to this book series: the books, like the exhibit, are truly collaborative projects.

I would particularly like to acknowledge the major contributions of:
Joanne Jones-Rizzi, who is profoundly dedicated to pluralism
Patricia Steuert, indefatigable leader of multiculturalism at
    The Children's Museum for the past twenty years
Diane Wachtell, our imaginative editor at The New Press

The following people gave crucial criticism and suggestions on the manuscript and design:
Abdus Muhammad, Annie Powell, Marco Torres, Terri Say, and their families;
Dorothy Merrill, Sylvia Sawin, Jeri Robinson, Kathryn Jones, Maria Cabrera,
Linda Warner, Dolores Calaf and Masa Sato.

The Kids Bridge exhibit was generously supported by:
Jessie B. Cox Charitable Trust
The Boston Foundation
Lotus Development Corporation
Digital Equipment Corporation
The Riley Foundation
The Xerox Foundation
Apple Computers, Inc., Community Affairs
The Foley, Hoag and Eliot Foundation

Hi! I'm Aylette, on the left. Here's Joanne, my friend and working partner, next to me. This story grew out of some adventures we had producing a video with a group of kids and grown-ups in our city, Boston, Massachusetts.

Our area turned out to be full of interesting neighborhoods and treasures that we want to share with you. Probably yours is, too, and we'll give you some ideas about how to explore your town. You'll find tips about making a video of your own, too.

Now, here are your guides for the trips you're about to take — Abdus, Annie, Marco, and Terri. They live in four different neighborhoods, and they'll take you to each one to look for some neat stuff. But you'll have to find the treasures yourself.

Here's a tip for your hunt. Be sure to go to the pages where the kids direct you, and you won't get lost.

Are you ready? Who would you like to go with first?

"Hi. Want to come to my part of town for rambutan? I'm Terri, and rambutan is a sweet fruit that some of us Cambodians love. You'll find me on page 8."

"Hola, I'm Marco! Come to my home for a snack of tostones. They're as good as French fries — and I love fries. My story begins on page 10."

"Hi there, I'm Annie. Want to see an Irish *claddagh* ring? You don't have to go to Ireland! I'll take you to find one near where I live, starting on page 27."

"Hey! Come with me, Abdus, to my neighborhood. We can get an African medallion like mine. Meet me on page 34."

And don't miss the end of the book. You can:

"Hi, I'm Terri. So you'd like to find some *rambutan*? If you want to see where to get it and how to prepare it, come with me. We videotaped a lot of Cambodians, like me, who live in my neighborhood. We have special stores here that sell things we're used to and we can't find any other place."

"Where would you like to start looking?"

"This is a place where Cambodian people can go for help and information. Check it out on page 21."

"Here's my favorite restaurant. They have really good Cambodian food here — and Chinese food, too. You'll find it on page 40."

"We get all kinds of Cambodian things in the Angkor Wat Market. You can hunt for rambutan in this store on page 24."

"This is a grocery store in my neighborhood. If you want to look for rambutan there, turn to page 38."

"*Hola*! Do you speak Spanish? `*Hola*´ means `hi,´ and you don't say the `h´—just say `ola´. Go on, try it."

"So you want to know about *tostones*? *Tostones* are fried plantains — *plátanos* in Spanish. We made a video in my neighborhood and my home so you can see what they are, and even how to make them. You can try it yourself — it's easy. And they're great!"

"First, I want to tell you about this place. We're in the plaza of Villa Victoria — it's the housing development where I live. Behind me is a mural that was made by some of the people of Villa Victoria to celebrate our Puerto Rican heritage. You can see some of the beautiful nature we have in Puerto Rico, one of our heroes, and — who's this? I guess you know who she is."

"Villa Victoria is a nice place to live — and not just for Latino people. We have an apartment building for elderly people who come from a mix of different backgrounds. Here in the plaza, lots of people sit around and talk, when it's warm weather."

11

Marco

Marco's parents are from Puerto Rico, a Caribbean island which is part of the United States. Like many Puerto Ricans, he and his family have traveled back and forth between Puerto Rico and Boston. He has relatives in both places, and both are "home" to him in some ways.

★ **PUERTO RICO** ★

You might be wondering — who are the "Latino" people Marco is talking about? They are all the Spanish-speaking people who live in Boston — they came originally from Puerto Rico, Cuba, El Salvador, Mexico — and a lot of other countries in the Caribbean and in Central and South America. And their cultures are different from each other in a lot of ways.

Are there Latino people in your area? Try asking your family or your teacher. The school system in your town or city probably knows where Latino kids live, and which cultural groups they belong to.

"Now, let's go to the market. You know, many of us Latinos speak Spanish to each other. But for this story, we'll just speak English, so you can understand if you don't know Spanish."

"*Hola*, Marco. What are you looking for?" asks Ismael, the store owner.

"I'm looking for *plátanos*. We're going to make *tostones*."

"Bueno. The *plátanos* are all the way in the back."

"This store has a lot of stuff. See those cans? The labels are in Spanish on one side and in English on the other. If you can find these in a store in your home town, you can teach yourself some Spanish. Can you find the *plátanos*?"

"Here they are. See, they look like bananas, only bigger. They're harder, too. Now, let's take them home. My mom will cook them."

"Ma, will you make tostones?" Marco asks. "What did you say?" she says slowly. "Pleeeeease?" "OK," says his mom, Carmen, smiling. "We'll do it together."

1

"Look," says Carmen, "this is how you do it. First I peel the *plátanos*."

2

"Then I cut them in slices. I have to be careful with the knife."

3

"Then I put them carefully in very hot vegetable oil and cook them until they're soft on the inside and golden on the outside."

"To test them, I take one out, and poke it with a fork. Sometimes, I taste one."

"Now, Marco, you put each one in the *tostonera,* and give it a good press to flatten it out a bit — that's right, press! If we didn't have a *tostonera*, we could use the bottom of a jar or a mug."

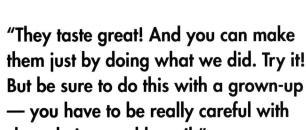

"Now I'm cooking them again — and after we drain them on paper towels and sprinkle them with a little salt, they're done."

"They taste great! And you can make them just by doing what we did. Try it! But be sure to do this with a grown-up — you have to be really careful with sharp knives and hot oil."

Marco

Snack Time

You may be able to find *plátanos,* or plantains, in a big supermarket in your town, but Latino markets are more fun to explore. See if you can find one. You'll probably see some delicious tropical fruits and juices, too. Here's a drink you can make to go with your *tostones.*

Batidas   (Fruit Shakes)

You'll need:
a blender
fresh fruit: either pineapple, bananas, mangoes, or oranges
milk or water
ice

Cut the fruit in small pieces and blend it with milk or water until it's smooth and bubbly. Pour into a glass over ice.

This is great to serve your friends, especially in the summer. And you've learned another Spanish word: *batidas,* pronounced ba-*tee*-das.

"OK, you who don't speak Spanish — how many new words have you learned? You should know `hola, tostones, bueno´ — that means `good´ — `plátanos,´ and `batidas.´ And here's a last one — *Adiós!* Bye!"

"Now, do you want to go to a different part of the city? Go back to page 7 and take a trip with Abdus, Terri, or Annie."

17

Marco

The Nubian Notion

"Good choice! This is a great place — it has all kinds of things about Africa and African-Americans."

"Do you have African medallions?"

"We sure do — they're in one of those baskets," Yvonne, the salesperson, answers.

"OK, it's up to you. Guess which basket!"

"Here it is, on the left — Did you guess right? Look at them all! Mine has a map of Africa on it; to me the black stands for black people like me, the green for the African land, and the red is for the blood of the people."

"If you haven't already explored the Museum of the National Center for Afro-American Artists, or the African Tropical Forest, you could turn back to pages 22 and 36."

"Or you can flip back to page 7 to hunt for a different something in a different neighborhood — with Annie, Marco, or Terri. Have fun!"

Abdus

Angkor Services

"Do you know where we could find *rambutan*?"

Mong Keo answers, "That's the first time I've ever been asked for that information! We help Cambodian people translate things they need to read, and we help them find apartments — that kind of thing. But I think I can tell you where to find *rambutan* — try the Angkor Wat Market up the street."

What if ...?

Imagine that you moved to a new country where you couldn't speak or read the language and everything was strange to you.

Think about some "simple" things you couldn't do;

- You wouldn't be able to read street signs, or anything else.

- You wouldn't be able to ask for anything in a store.

- You wouldn't know how to get around in a neighborhood — much less go to other neighborhoods.

- And the school would probably be completely different from your old school — and of course, all the kids would be strange to you.

You'd probably be glad to find someone from your own country who could help you figure things out.

"Guess you'll have to go back to page 9 and try another place."

21

Terri

Museum of the National Center for Afro-American Artists

"Here we are, in front of the Museum of the National Center for Afro-American Artists. Isn't that a serious name! Actually, it's a pretty serious place; they show paintings and other artwork by people of color, like me. Isn't this sculpture amazing? It's made of bronze and it's called `Eternal Presence´."

"Let's look in the museum shop and you can see if they have medallions."

If Abdus is a kid from the United States, why all this talk about Africa?

Like other people, many African-Americans are very proud of their heritage. Their African ancestors were captured and brought to this country as slaves nearly four hundred years ago. They were torn away from their homes, their families, their leaders, their work, their arts. They weren't allowed to carry much with them except what was in their heads. Their memories were strong, and they worked very hard, often against the wishes of their slavemasters, to continue some of their culture here. Today many African-American people know a lot about the arts and ways of life in Africa, and this has become an important part of their life here. It reminds them of their African heritage and their connections with African peoples and their descendents all around the world.

How about you?

Where did your ancestors come from?
How did they get here?

Can you find anything in your home that shows where your people came from? It might be something passed down in your family from one generation to another, or it might be something that was bought because it's connected to your heritage — like a special cooking implement, or a picture on the wall. See what you can find!

"All these things were made in Africa. African artists and craftspeople use wood, metal, grasses, cloth — all kinds of things — to make this beautiful stuff to wear, to use, and to enjoy. See any medallions?"

"No medallions here! Guess we'll have to look somewhere else. How about trying the Nubian Notion on page 18; or the African Tropical Forest on page 36."

the Nubian Notion on page 18; or the African Tropical Forest on page 36.

Abdus

Angkor Wat Market

"OK, now I'm going to tell you, I think they really do have *rambutan* in this store. In this store they sell blankets and clothes and cooking stuff and fresh fruits and fish and vegetables — almost everything we Cambodians use."

"So, can you find the *rambutan*?"

"See the incense sticks? We use this in our temple, or in a home shrine — we're Buddhists. It smells nice, like roses, jasmine, and other kinds of flowers. And here's a little statue of the Buddha. These dishes were made in China. That prickly fruit is called a *durian*."

"See the *rambutan*?

Let's go get my aunt to
prepare it — she lives near here."

"*Rambutan* has a kind of rough shell.
First we cut it, then we peel it off. The
fruit inside is soft and sweet."

25

Terri

"Most of us are related to each other in this building, so when we have something special, a lot of the kids show up!"

"These are really good. If there's an Asian store in your town, ask for rambutan. I bet you'd like them."

"If you missed some stores in my neighborhood, look on pages 21, 38, and 40."

"Or go back to page 7 to find some more good stuff in other neighborhoods. Me, I'm off to get a hamburger — I'm still hungry!"

Terri

"Hi, I'm Annie. Glad you found me. My grandparents came from Ireland, and I've wanted an Irish *claddagh* ring for a really long time. This is what they look like. We videotaped my trip around my neighborhood to find one. I'm glad you want to come along. By the way, if you say `claddagh` out loud, don't say the `gh` — it's pronounced `clad-a`. Got it?"

A N N i e

"I have to check in at home before we go shopping. You can meet my family."

"Hi, Annie," her mom says. "What's up?"

"Hi, Mom, hi, Dad, hi, David," Annie says. "I've saved up enough money, and I want to go and buy my *claddagh* ring. Today. Right now."

"Oh, oh," says her dad. "Now maybe we'll know if you've got a secret boyfriend. You know, if you wear a *claddagh* ring with the heart pointing toward you, it's supposed to mean you've got a sweetheart, and if it's pointing away, it means you don't."

"Now don't tease her, Dad," says her mother. "Annie, you can go today, but I'd like you to do an errand for me first. This morning when I went to Mass, Father Burns said there are thirty people in the homeless shelter right now. I'd like you to get some bread and take it over to St. Ambrose Church for them."

"OK, Mom," Annie answers. "I'll go to the Keltic Krust — they have the best bread. And I can say hello to my friend Caroline."

"I wish you could smell this place — it's delicious. There are all kinds of Irish breads and pastries here."

"Hi, Annie, what can I do for you?" asks Caroline.

"Hi, Caroline. Can I have four loaves of Irish brown bread? Caroline, I'm going to get a *claddagh* ring today, I've finally got enough money. Do you have one?"

"Yes, I do," says Caroline. "I got it at the Card Fair. I really love it."

"Caroline, you've got the heart pointing toward you. Does that mean you've got a boyfriend?"

"I'll never tell!" Caroline answers with a smile.

"Father Burns, I've brought some bread for the families in the shelter."

"Thank you, Annie," Father Burns answers. "It's so appropriate you should be bringing bread, because the reading at this afternoon's Mass was about Jesus feeding the people who were hungry — and we have many hungry people in our city even today. Now what are you up to?"

"I'm on my way to the Card Fair shop to get a *claddagh* ring."

"Ah," says Father Burns smiling, "now we'll find out if you've a boyfriend."

"Oh, Father," Annie answers, "I'm not so interested in boyfriends, you know. I have a few other things on my mind, after all."

"This is the Card Fair. Irish-Americans, like me, especially like to shop here because there are a lot of special things from Ireland. Now let's see if we can find a *claddagh* ring."

"May I see a *claddagh* ring?" Annie asks.

"Certainly," Eileen, the salesperson, answers. "We have gold *claddagh* rings, and we have sterling silver *claddagh* rings. Do you know the old story of the *claddagh* rings?"

Annie shakes her head. "Well, long ago, when there was a famine in Ireland, a husband would leave his wife and children in Ireland to find a better life in America. The man would give his wife a *claddagh* ring, and she would give him a *claddagh* ring. The heart means love, the hands mean friendship, and the crown means loyalty. Hearts and hands across the sea.

Today there's a different meaning. I see you've put on the ring with the heart pointing toward you. Do you have a boyfriend?"

Annie answers with a smile, "I'll never tell!"

What's behind the old story about the *claddagh* ring?

People have been coming from Ireland to the United States for the past four hundred years. They, like most immigrants, have come for a lot of different reasons, and like other immigrants, some of them had a hard time when they first got here.

IRELAND

Now that so many Irish-Americans have good jobs and are comfortably settled here, this seems hard to imagine. In Boston, for example, many Irish have become important politicians and other leaders. And of course, President John F. Kennedy was an Irish-American.

If your family came here from another country a long time ago, you might want to find out how they were treated when they first came. And when you meet new immigrants, you could think about how they're being treated now. Do they have a hard time getting jobs? Do some people treat them badly? We can all work to help new Americans feel welcome and comfortable here, as many of us have become.

The story of the *claddagh* ring that Eileen told Annie in the Card Fair shop refers to a time over a hundred years ago when the farm crops in Ireland — mainly potatoes — didn't grow well. Many families depended on potatoes as their main food, and so they went hungry and many even starved to death. This is called a famine. Many people came to the United States to make a better life. Often a father would come first and try to earn enough money to support his family in Ireland and to pay for their travel to the United States. But here some people treated the Irish badly. Some people who were hiring workers would put out a sign that said, "No Irish Need Apply," because they were prejudiced and didn't like Irish workers.

"OK, you've found my ring, but not my secret. Now go back to page 7 and either Marco, Abdus, or Terri will take you to find a different treasure."

"Hi. I got my medallion right here in my part of town. You can find a medallion in one of the three places that we videotaped — what's your best guess?"

"This is the Museum of the National Center for Afro-American Artists. If you want to look in their shop, go to page 22."

"Do you think the African Tropical Forest in the Boston Zoo would be a good place? Look on page 36."

"You can check out a store called the Nubian Notion — you'll see it on page 18."

African Tropical Forest

"Here I am in the African Tropical Forest exhibit in the Boston Zoo — and it's right in *my* neighborhood, Roxbury. Videotaping it in here is pretty amazing — it looks and smells and sounds like a really tropical place — and check out these animals! Can you see the hippo? I guess this is what the jungle must be like in Africa."

Do you think Africa is all jungle?

In fact, less than a tenth of Africa is tropical forest. Africa has deserts and grasslands and even snowy mountaintops! People have a lot of mixed-up ideas about Africa. Do you know that there are many cities in Africa the size of U.S. cities? Brazzaville in the Congo and Nairobi, Kenya, both have about half a million people — about the size of Boston. Mamputo, Mozambique, has more than 750,000 people, just like Baltimore, Maryland. And more than one million people live in Lagos, Nigeria, and in San Diego, California. In Africa, there are skyscrapers, and apartment houses, suburbs, and farmhouses. In fact, a lot of Africans have houses and schools that are probably much like yours.

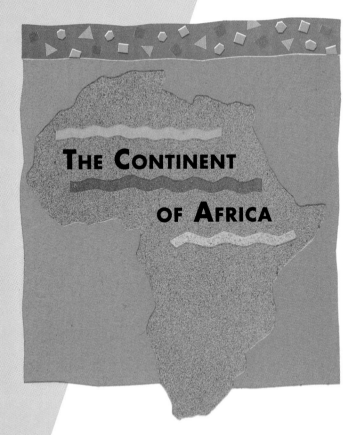

THE CONTINENT OF AFRICA

"Guess I kind of tricked you on this one — it's all about Africa, but they don't sell African medallions here. How about trying The Museum of the National Center for Afro-American Artists on page 22 or the Nubian Notion on page 18."

Abdus

Myer's Kosher Kitchen

"Here we are in Myer's Kosher Kitchen. Let's see what we can find."

"Hello. Do you sell *rambutan*?"

"We don't have *rambutan* — this is a kosher market," Gary Kaplan, the owner, answers with a surprised look. "We have a variety of Jewish foods — we have *knishes*, which are meat- or potato-filled pastries, we have *kishka*, which is like a sausage, and we have stuffed cabbage. We do have a Chinese-style egg roll — but you'll have to look somewhere else for *rambutan*."

38

Southeast Asians: Some of the Newest Immigrants

Southeast Asians have been coming to the United States for almost twenty years from Vietnam, Cambodia, and Laos. They have left their lands because the wars in their countries have been so terrible.

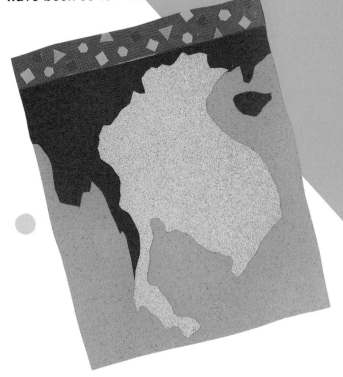

Many had to leave their homes with very little money and few possessions. Sometimes families couldn't even stay together. Here in the United States they are working very hard to get settled, to learn English, to get jobs, to learn about this country, and to keep their own culture alive. Now that so many Southeast Asians live here, we can learn about their beautiful crafts, their games and foods, their music, dance, and their way of life. They aren't a single cultural group either — there are Vietnamese, Cambodians, Laotians, Khmu, and Hmong, each with different languages and life-styles.

Are there Southeast Asian people in your community?

A Jewish Market in a Cambodian Neighborhood?

A lot of different ethnic groups have settled in Terri's neighborhood over the years. This kosher market is a reminder of a time when mostly Jewish people lived here. Are there neighborhoods in your town which have been home to many different groups over time?

"Guess I was trying to fool you on this one. Better try the next page. Or pick a different place on page 9."

39

Terri

Phnom Penh Restaurant

"Hello, Terri, what do you want today?" asks Hong Taing in Khmer, the language of Cambodia.

"I'm looking for *rambutan*," says Terri.

"We don't have any," he says. "We have all kinds of meat, fish, and vegetable and rice and noodle dishes — but no *rambutan*. Sorry."

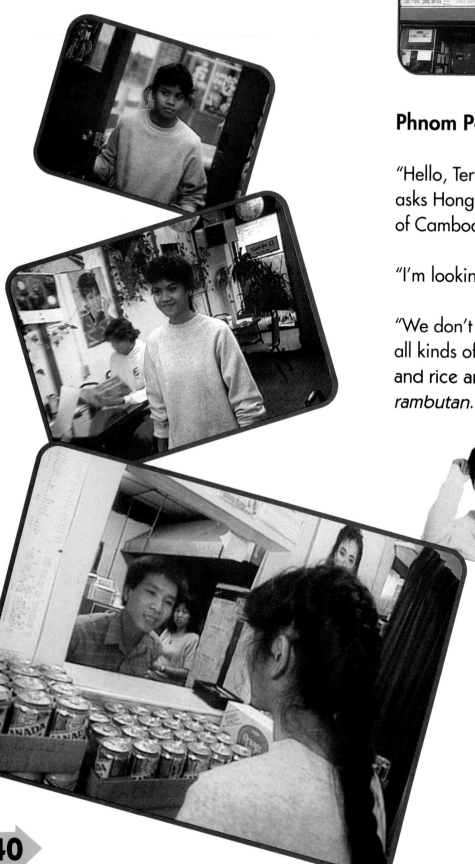

Learning a New Language

When Terri came to the United States nine years ago, she didn't speak any English. She spoke Khmer. She learned English quickly by talking to kids and studying hard in school. Now she can even read and write in English.

But her own first language, Khmer, is still important to her. It's a part of her culture, like the Cambodian food she likes. She speaks Khmer to her family and friends a lot.

You know, if you hear people around you speaking a language you don't understand, you may imagine they're talking about you, or saying something they don't want you to understand. But they're probably just talking about the same sorts of things you talk about with your friends and family.

Guess how many languages are spoken in the area around Boston: 5? 31? 95? 17? The answer is 17! How many languages do you think are spoken in your area? You can probably find out at your school.

Do you speak more than one language? If you're studying a new language in school, you know how hard it is to learn.

"Guess you'll have to go back to page 9 and try another place."

Terri

How well do you know Abdus, Annie, Marco and Terri?
Here's a quiz for you.

1. Who loves French fries?

2. Who sometimes eats hamburgers?

3. Who showed us what comic strip character?

4. Where did the kids' families, or their ancestors, come from?

5. Whose family has been here the longest?

6. Who arrived most recently?

7. Who speaks another language besides English?

Answers

1. Marco — and he loves *tostones*, too. 2. Terri. She doesn't eat just Cambodian food! 3. Marco: Lucy is on the mural in Villa Victoria. 4. Annie's came from Ireland, Marco's from Puerto Rico, Abdus's from Africa, and Terri's from Cambodia 5. Abdus's ancestors — Africans were brought as slaves to the United States starting in the 1600s. 6. Terri's: her family came here in the 1980s. 7. Terri speaks Khmer, though she's forgetting a lot of it, and Marco speaks Spanish.

How'd you do?

What About You?

Where did your family come from before they settled here? What special foods do you have? Do you wear things that belong to your cultural group?

What about your neighborhood?

Exploring neighborhoods is fun, and you could start with your own. You might find some surprises! In your neighborhood, are most of the people from the same cultural group? Or are the people in your neighborhood very different from each other?

Can you find out what countries your neighbors originally came from? What languages are spoken in your neighborhood? Do your neighbors have special things like Annie's *claddagh* ring and Abdus's medallion? Or special foods like Terri and Marco?

43

Exploring New Neighborhoods

Have you ever explored neighborhoods different from your own?

You may have heard that some neighborhoods in your town or city are dangerous or unfriendly or boring. These reports could be exaggerated. You can have wonderful experiences in unfamiliar neighborhoods if you go about it carefully. Here are some tips:

Always plan explorations with the grown-ups in your family; you'll need their help with these adventures.

Going into an unfamiliar neighborhood is a little like going into someone's home. It *is* home to the people who live there. You'll want to be as polite, friendly, and respectful as you would if you went into someone's house.

The very best way to get to know a new neighborhood is to make a connection with people living there. Do you have a friend who lives in a different part of your town? You could get to know each other's neighborhoods. If you belong to a group like the scouts, you might be able to get together with a troop in the neighborhood you want to explore. Or maybe your school could have pen pals in a school in that neighborhood, and then you could visit. If you belong to an afterschool program, perhaps you could exchange visits with an afterschool program in another neighborhood: you could invite them to your neighborhood and show them around, and you could visit theirs. Your church might have a connection with a church in another neighborhood.

You could also go into public places in a new neighborhood — like a restaurant, a shop, or the library. You could see if there are neighborhood festivals where everyone is welcome. If you go into a store or restaurant in a neighborhood that's new to you, say **hello** first. You could say you don't know a lot about their place, but you want to learn. You can ask questions in a polite way about things you see; often people like to explain about their specialties. If they don't want to talk a lot, don't worry; some people are quiet, or it may be because you don't speak their language, and they don't speak much English. Or they're just too busy. Sometimes kids help their families in neighborhood stores, and you might be able to get to know them — just like you got to know Abdus, Annie, Terri, and Marco.

Making a Video

The video in this book was made by professional film people, but if you can use a camcorder, **you** can make a video of your neighborhood treasures or those in other neighborhoods. This can be a school, afterschool, or club project. You can write your own story, too, to share with other kids. Maybe you can read this book to younger children in your school or afterschool program and show them your video and tell them about it.

Here are some hints from D'Arcy Marsh, the director/cameraperson who worked on our video.

Plan on making a short video; fifteen minutes is plenty for people to watch and for you to plan.

Research your area for treasures and places to go. It's important to do this before you start filming. Make a long list, then choose the best. If you plan to video people, be sure to tell them about your project and ask their permission. Some people may not want to be filmed, so you need to have enough choices.

Write down an outline of your video; list each place in the order that you want it to be in your video story. Probably showing five places and interviewing five people will be plenty.

"Good luck, guys!"

"Hope you find some good stuff."

Then plan your story boards; that means a shot by shot list, with how long you want each shot to take. — Think about the beginning; how do you want to start the video? Maybe a shot of a main street, or a well-known place? Will you have someone speaking to the camera saying what this video is about? — How will you announce each location? Again, you can interview someone who'll explain where you are. — How will you end the video? You could show the treasures you've found and brought back with you.

Now add up your times; if you've run over fifteen minutes, cut some of it back. You're ready for tryout; do a small part of the video, and see how it looks. Get some advice, too. Here are some general tips for videotaping: — always move the camera slowly and smoothly; — keep the lens wide open, unless you're pretty skillful at close-ups; — videotape where there's enough light.

This sounds pretty complicated, but it's a lot of fun. Give it a try!

"Hope you make friends!"

Adiós!"

47

Glossary

Here are definitions for some words and phrases in this book which you may not already know.

ancestors:
people from whom your family came way back in time, like your grandparents' grandparents.

Buddhists:
people all over the world who follow Buddhism, a major religion started in Asia by Buddha.

camcorder:
a lightweight television camera and videocassette recorder.

claddagh ring:
an Irish ring standing for love, friendship, and loyalty.

cultural group:
people sharing a similar way of life, which may include such things as beliefs, customs, values, foods, arts, language, etc.

descendents:
people who trace their families back to a particular person or group.

ethnic groups:
people sharing a particular racial, national, religious and/or language heritage.

festival:
a gathering by a group of people to celebrate something, often on a regular basis.

generation:
referring to the time between the birth of parents and the birth of their children. Your parents are one generation, and you're the next generation.

heritage:
things and customs handed down from earlier generations.

immigrant:
a person who leaves one country to settle in another.

kosher:
food which is prepared according to particular Jewish religious rules.

medallion:
a circular design used as decoration.

prejudice:
an attitude formed without enough previous knowledge or thought.

rambutan: a sweet fruit grown in hot climates.

tostones:
fried slices of plantain, a tropical fruit somewhat like bananas.

tostonera:
a wooden press for flattening slices of plantain.